Develop Snakes & Ladders Game Complete Guide with Code & Design

Anurag Pandey

Published by Anurag Pandey, 2023.

While every precaution has been taken in the preparation of this book, the publisher assumes no responsibility for errors or omissions, or for damages resulting from the use of the information contained herein.

DEVELOP SNAKES & LADDERS GAME COMPLETE GUIDE WITH CODE & DESIGN

First edition. April 9, 2023.

ISBN: 979-8215863473

Written by Anurag Pandey.

Table of Contents

Preface

Develop Snakes & Ladders Game

Complete Guide with Code & Design

With help of design support & code given in above book, you will be able to develop your own Snakes & Ladders Game instantly. In addition to fixed snakes and ladders, the game features two automated escalators, which dramatically send the player up and down.

However Design and Code given in this book are complete and need no modification, but you can also improvise them.

If you are a beginner then this book will help you to learn coding, logic building and applying methods in programming.

You should be at least little familiar with Visual Basic.

So we shall develop our VB based Snakes & Ladders game now:

Design Guide

Step 1:

Open Visual Basic and create New Project.

Screenshot: 1

Step 2:

Save Form1.frm

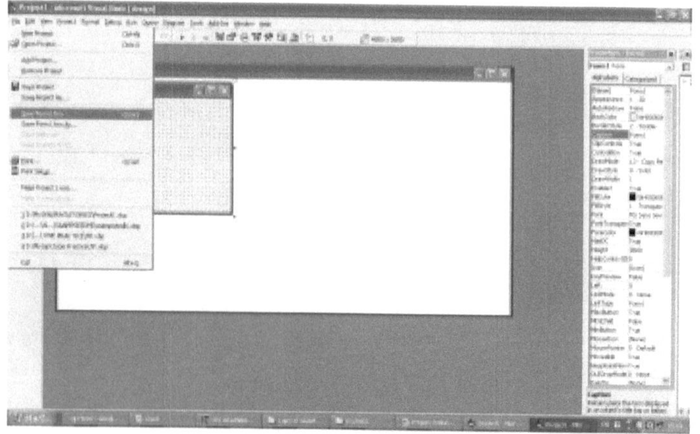

Screenshot: 2

Step 3:

Name it or let it be default "Form1"

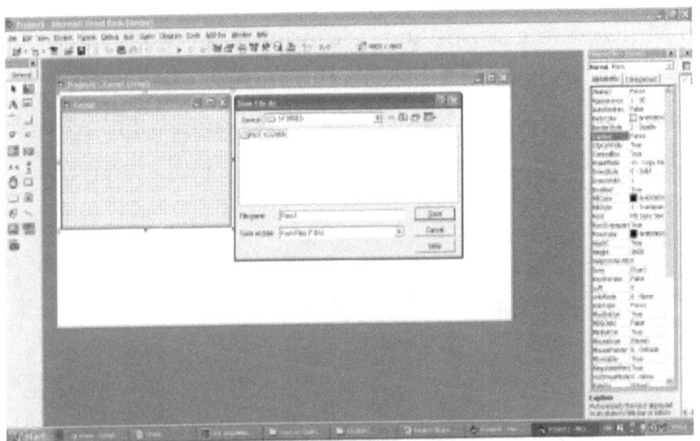

Screenshot: 3

Step 4:

Save Project the same way

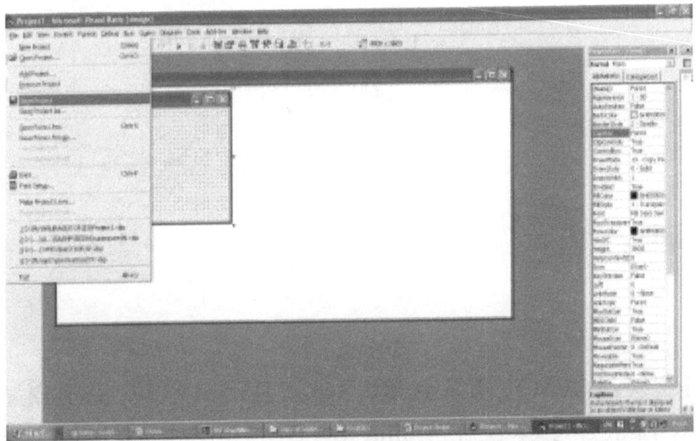

Screenshot: 4

Step 5:

Capture 10 pictures given below and make jpg files as per given instruction. If you have eBook then using Copy or Print Screen Paste them to MSPaint one by one and save as jpg files.

Image 1: SNAKE-BACKGROUND.jpg [It will be used as Background image of VB Form1. Logic of Game is linked with boxes drawn on this image, so you have to use this or similar image.]

Image: 1

IMPORTANT ABOUT BACKGROUND IMAGE: Save this image with any name.jpg or background.jpg. This image Pixels must be 825 Width X 660 Height. So you have to resize this picture with help of some app or do like this. Open this Image with Microsoft Office Picture Manager - Click on Edit Pictures - Click on Resize - Select Custom Width X Height – Enter Width = 825 and Height = 660 – Click on

OK – Save the Image. DONE. We don't need to resize other images. You may need to resize button.jpg.

Image 2: PAASE1.JPG [It will be used as Picture of Image1(0)]

Image: 2

Image 3: PAASE2.JPG [It will be used as Picture of Image1(1)]

Image: 3

Image 4: PAASE3.JPG [It will be used as Picture of Image1(2)]

Image: 4

Image 5: PAASE4.JPG [It will be used as Picture of Image1(3)]

Image: 5

Image 6: PAASE5.JPG [It will be used as Picture of Image1(4)]

Image: 6

Image 7: PAASE6.JPG [It will be used as Picture of Image1(5)]

Image: 7

Image 8: Cone1.jpg [It will be used as Picture of Image2(0)]

Image: 8

Image 9: Cone2.jpg [It will be used as Picture of Image2(1)]

Image: 9

Image 10: Button.jpg [It will be used as Picture of Command Button Command1(0)]

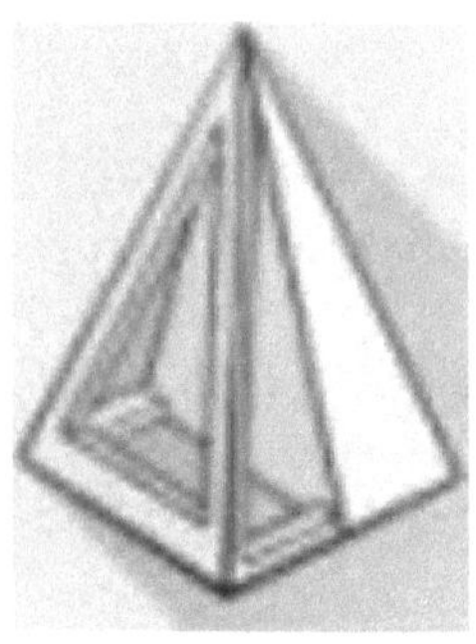

Image: 10

Step 6:

Now we have to design our VB Form as shown in Screenshot: 5.

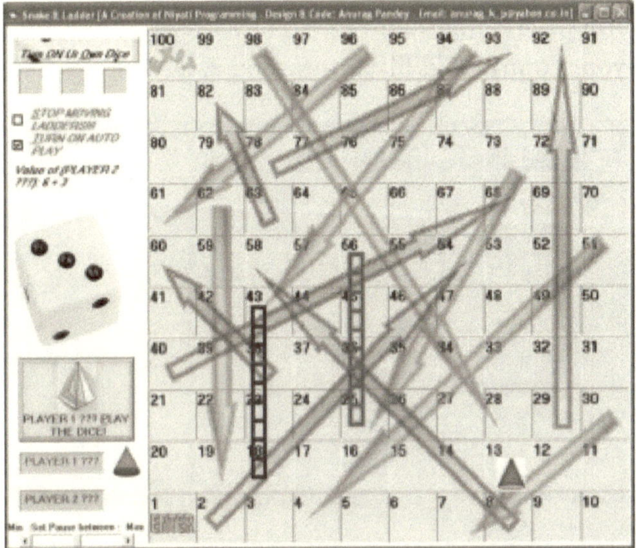

Screenshot: 5

Confused?

Let me clear you.

Here looks your Form1 now as shown in Screenshot: 6.

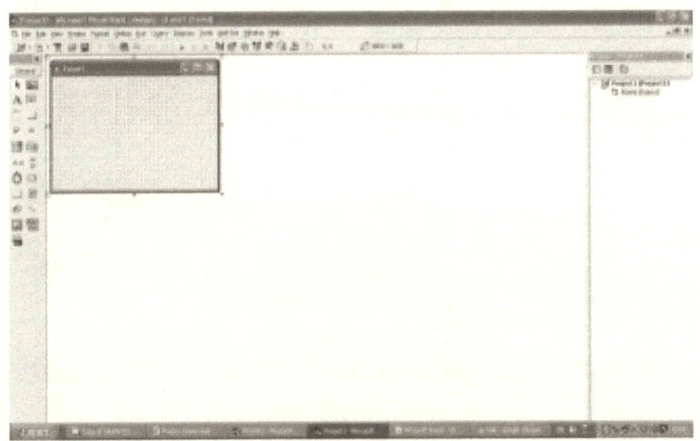

Screenshot: 6

Set Form1 width = 12525

　　Set Form1 height = 10500

　　Set Form1 StartUpPosition = 2- CenterScreen

　　Now your Form1 looks like Screenshot: 7.

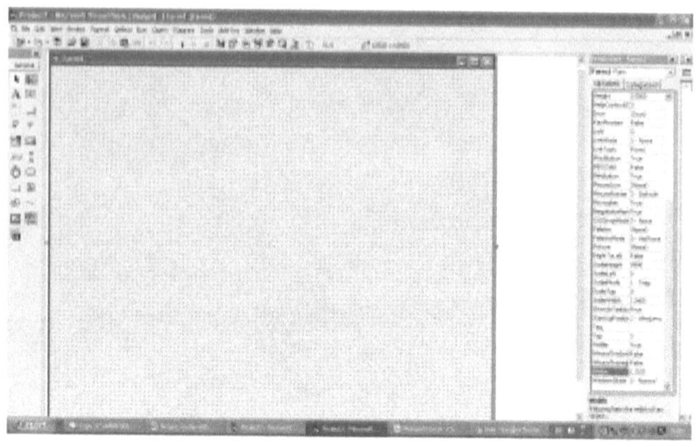

Screenshot: 7

Now Set Form1 Picture = SNAKE-BACKGROUND.jpg image

　　First set the background image to the form. Then your Form1 would look like Screenshot: 8.

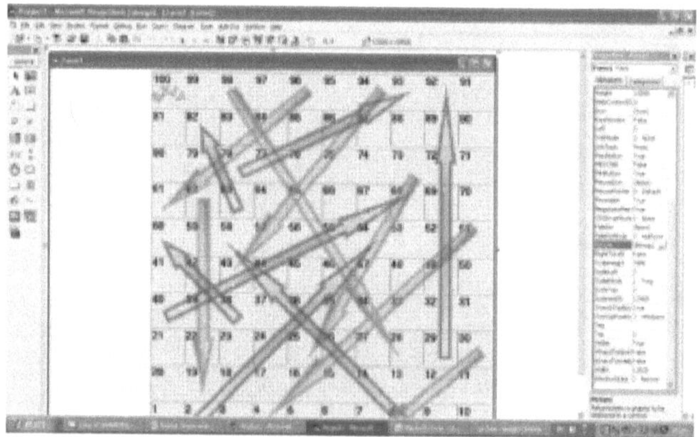

Screenshot: 8

Now we shall add following controls one by one.

First of all we shall add Array of Command Buttons. There are two Command Buttons – Command1(0) and Command1(1)

Screenshot: 9

PLAY THE DICE is an array of command button Command1. Name it Command1(0).

    Set Command1(0) Top = 6360
    Set Command1(0) Left = 240
    Set Command1(0) Height = 1575
    Set Command1(0) Width = 2295

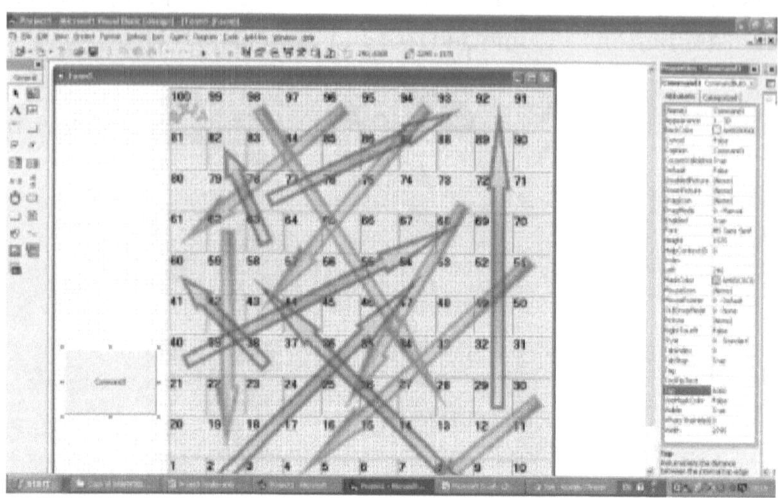

Screenshot: 10

Set Command1(0) Caption = "&PLAY THE DICE"

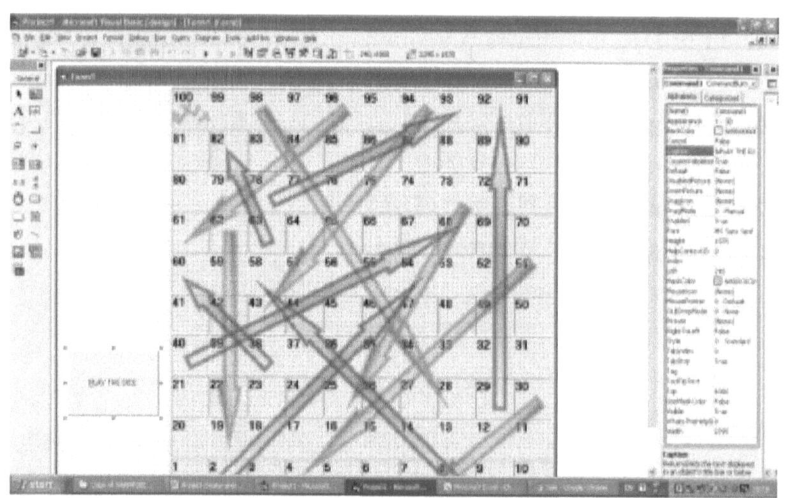

Screenshot: 11

Set Command1(0) Backcolor = &H0080FF80&

Set Command1(0) Style = 1 – Graphical

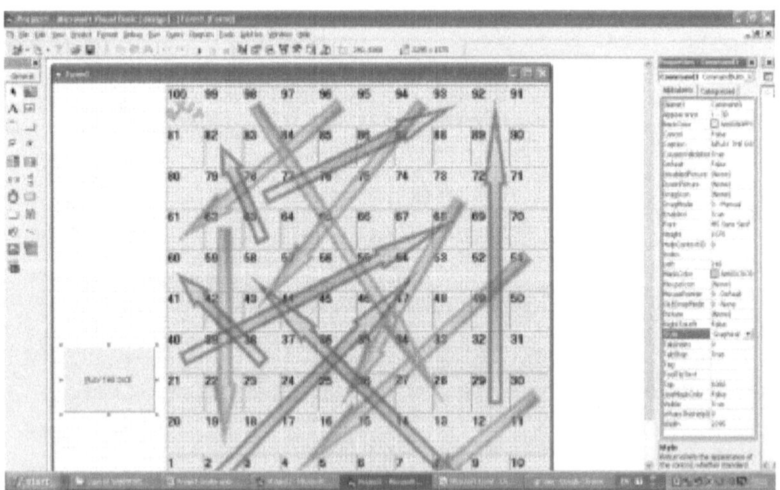

Screenshot: 12

Set Command1(0) Picture = Button.jpg image

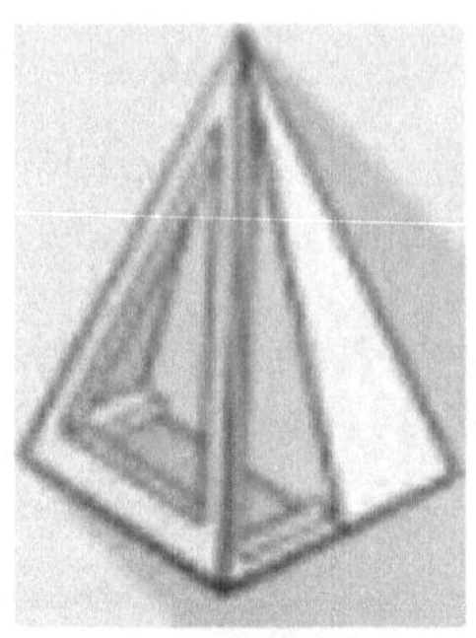

Now Form1 would look like Screenshot: 13

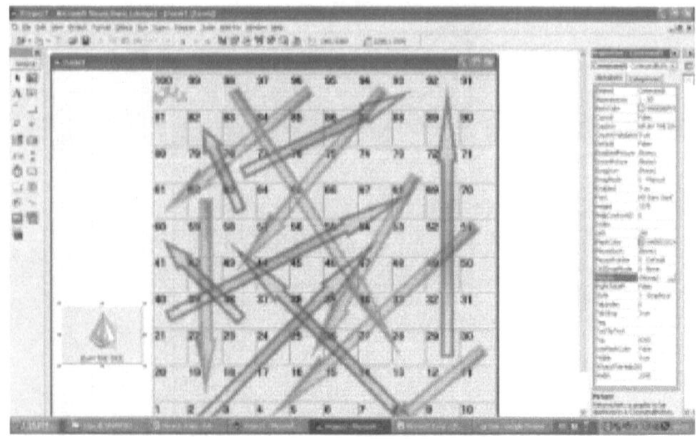

Screenshot: 13

Now we shall add Command1(1). At present Command1(0) Name is "Command1". Now we shall make array of this. Select Command1, then Right Click then Copy. Then Paste.

A Message Box will appear – You already have a control named "Command1". Do you want to create a control array?

Click on Yes. Now you have two Command buttons – Commaqnd1(0) and Command1(1) as shown in Screenshot: 14.

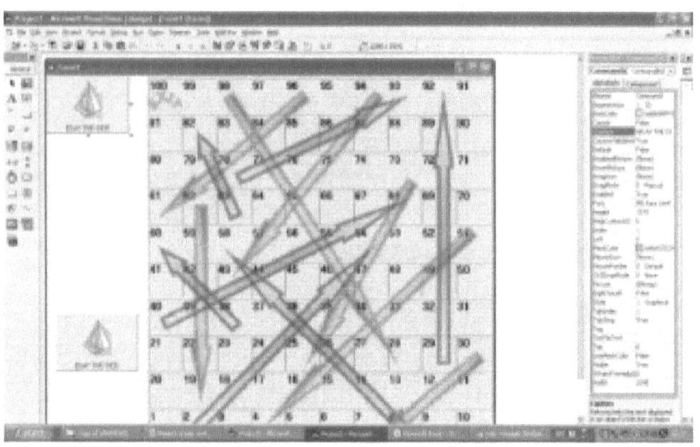

Screenshot: 14

Set Command1(1) Caption = "Turn ON Ur &Own Dice"

Set Command1(1) Top = 240

Set Command1(1) Left = 120

Set Command1(1) Height = 495

Set Command1(1) Width = 2535

You can set Command1(1) Picture of your choice. Now Form1 would look like Screenshot: 15.

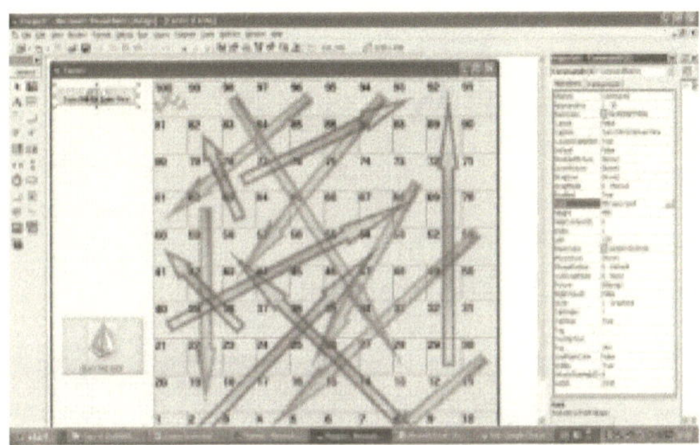

Screenshot: 15

Now we shall add Image Control.

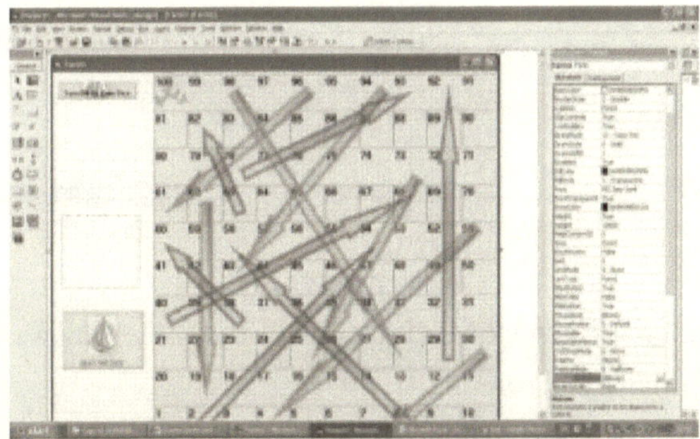

Screenshot: 16

Set Image1(0) Top = 3600

Set Image1(0) left = 120

Set Image1(0) Height = 2745

Set Image1(0) Width = 2370

Set Image1(0) Visible = False

Set Image1(0) Picture = Passe1.jpg

Now Form1 would look like Screenshot: 17

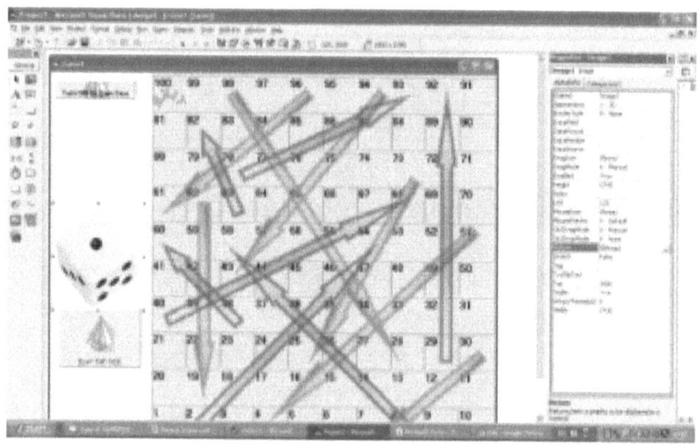

Screenshot: 17

Now we shall create array of Image control the same way we had created array of Command Button.

Select Image Control then Right Click then Copy then Paste then Click on Yes.

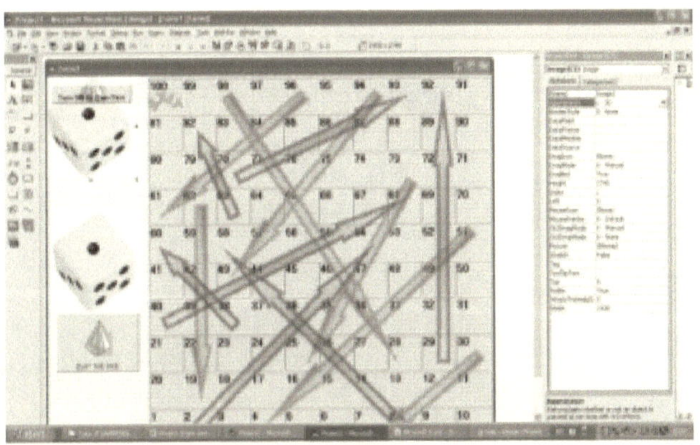

Screenshot: 18

Repeat this until you get total Six Image Controls. They will have names Image1(0), Image1(1), Image1(2), Image1(3), Image1(4) and Image1(5).

Set Image1(1) Picture = Paase2.jpg

Set Image1(2) Picture = Paase3.jpg

Set Image1(3) Picture = Paase4.jpg

Set Image1(4) Picture = Paase5.jpg

Set Image1(5) Picture = Paase6.jpg

Now form1 would look like Screenshot: 19.

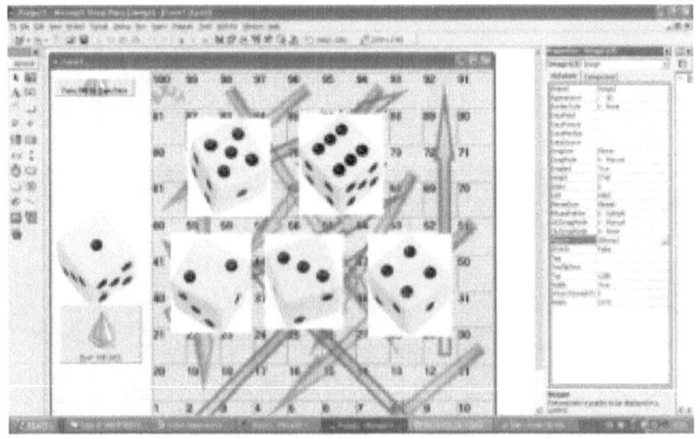

Screenshot: 19

Now set Top and Left of all Image same to Image1(0). Now your Form1 would look like Screenshot: 20.

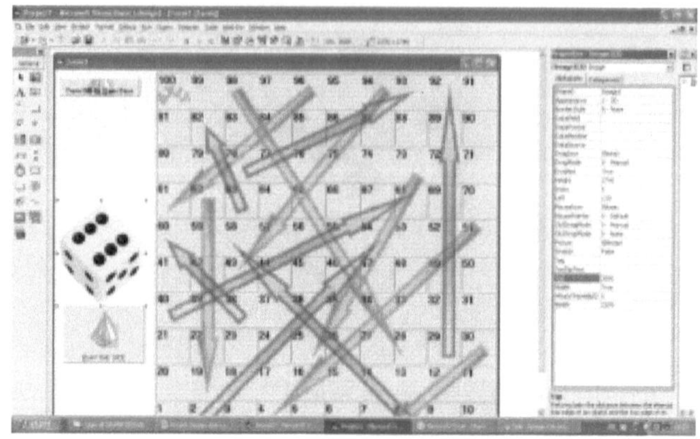

Screenshot: 20

Now we shall add Textbox Control as shown in Screenshot: 21

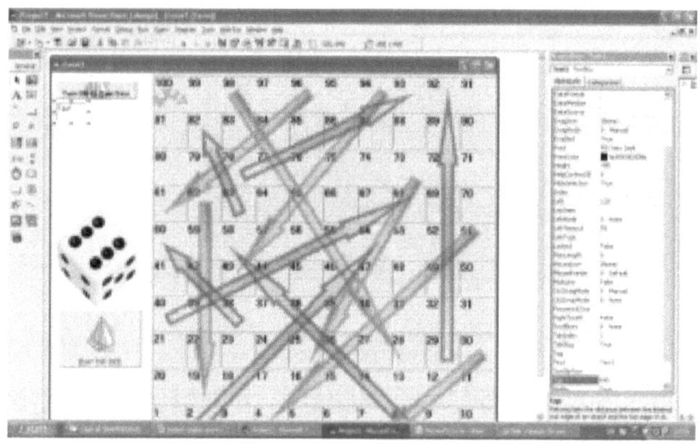

Screenshot: 21

Set Text1 Text = ""

Set Text1 Enabled = FALSE

Set Text1 Height = 495

Set Text1 Width = 495

Set Text1 Top = 840

Set Text1 Left = 240

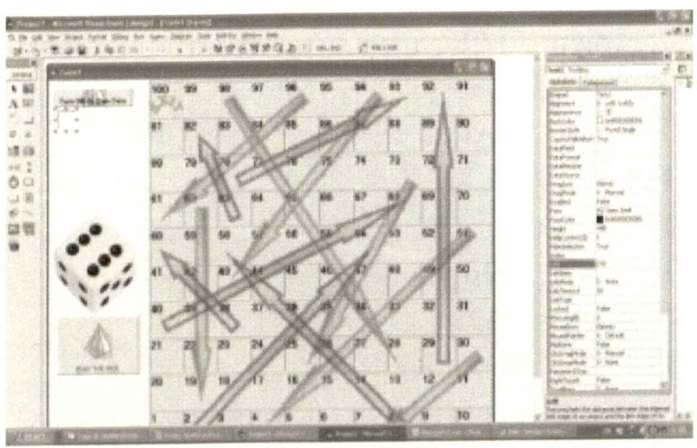

Screenshot: 22

Now create array of Textbox. Create three Textboxes, Text1(0), Text1(1) and Text1(2) as shown in Screenshot: 23

Set Text1(1) Left = 1080

Set Text1(2) Left = 1920

Now Form1 would look like Screenshot: 23.

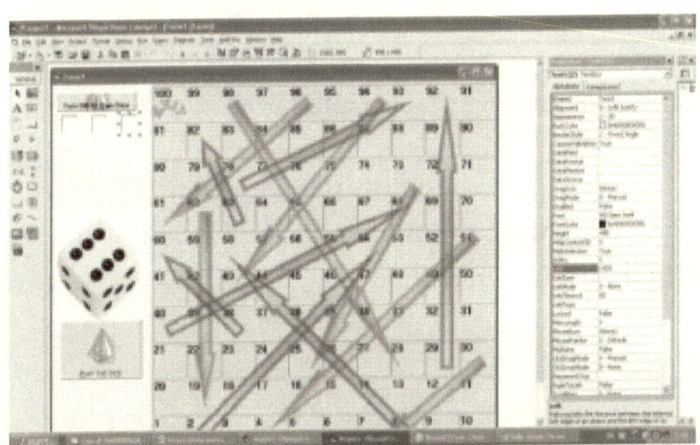

Screenshot: 23

Now we shall create Array of two Textbox the same way, Text2(0) and Text2(1).

Text2(0) Top = 8160

Text2(0) Left = 240
Text2(0) Height = 420
Text2(0) Width = 1695
Text2(0) Text = "PLAYER 1 ???"
Text2(1) Top = 8880
Text2(1) Left = 240
Text2(1) Height = 420
Text2(1) Width = 1695
Text2(1) Text = "PLAYER 2 ???"
Now your Form1 would look like Screenshot: 24

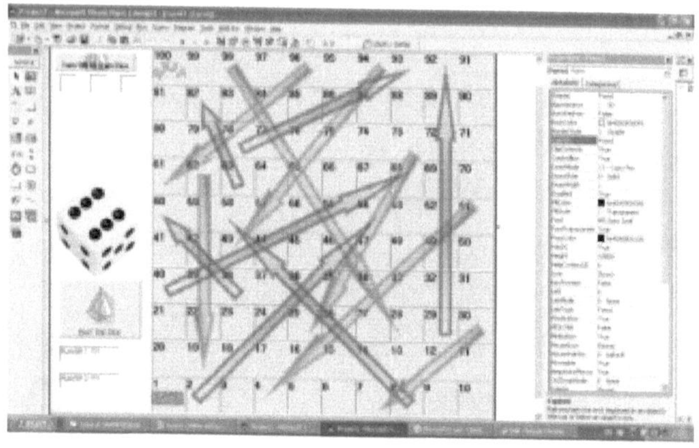

Screenshot: 24

Now we shall add Array of another Image Control – Image2(0) and Image2(1) as shown in Screenshot: 25

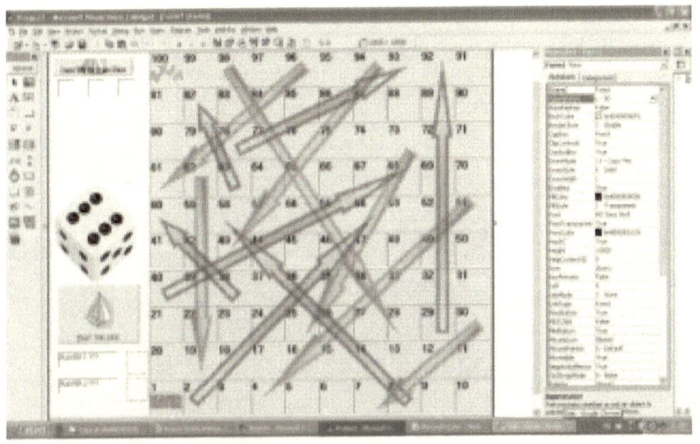

Screenshot: 25

Set Image2(0) Picture = Cone1.jpg

Set Image2(1) Picture = Cone2.jpg

Set Image2(0) Top = 8040
   Set Image2(0) Left = 2100

Set Image2(0) Height = 615
Set Image2(0) Width = 555
Set Image2(0) Stretch = True
Set Image2(1) Top = 8760
Set Image2(1) Left = 2100
Set Image2(1) Height = 645
Set Image2(1) Width = 570
Set Image2(1) Stretch = True
Now Form1 would look like Screenshot: 26.

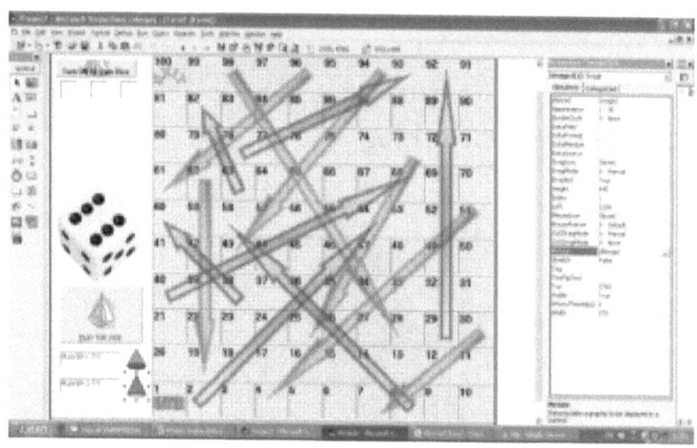

Screenshot: 26

Now Add Label Control named Label1(0) below with below properties
Label1(0). Caption = "Min :Set Pause between : Max"
Label1(0) Top = 9480
Label1(0) Left = 0
Label1(0) Height = 195
Label1(0) Width = 2730
Label1(0) BackStyle = 0- Transparent
Now Form1 would look like Screenshot: 27

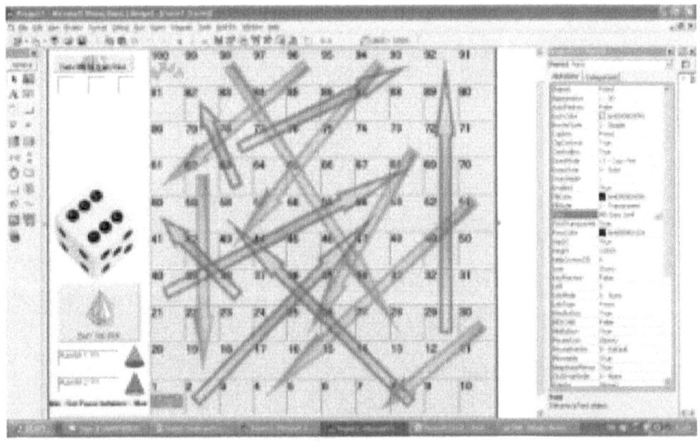

Screenshot: 27

Same way add Label1(1) with properties like below

  Label1(1). Caption = "Value :"

  Label1(1) Top = 2640

  Label1(1) Left = 120

  Label1(1) Height = 615

  Label1(1) Width = 2415

  Label1(1) BackStyle = 0- Transparent

Now Form1 would look like Screenshot: 28

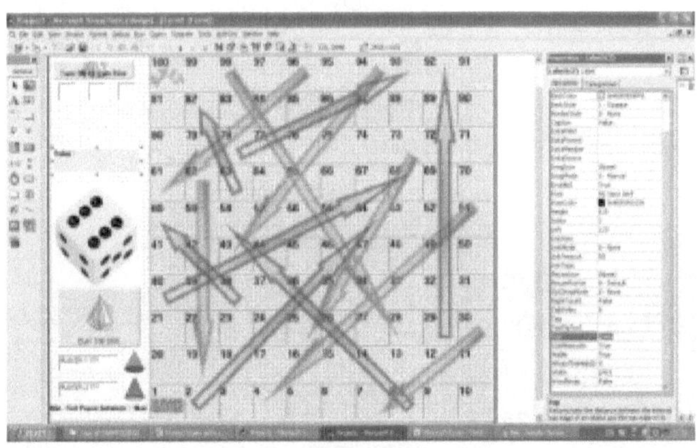

Screenshot: 28

BackStyle property of Label1(0) and Label1(1) are set later as Transparent. Now same way we shall add Label1(2) with properties like below:

Label1(2). Caption = ""
Label1(2) BackColor = &H00FFFFC0&
Label1(2) Top = 2040
Label1(2) Left = 4680
Label1(2) Height = 5895
Label1(2) Width = 6615
Label1(2) Visible = FALSE
Now Form1 would look like Screenshot: 29

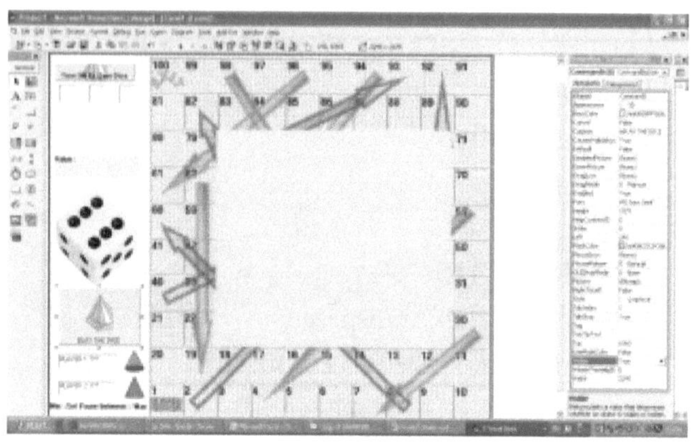

Screenshot: 29

Now we shall add two Checkboxes

Check1 and Check2 with below properties
Check1 Caption = "&TURN ON AUTO PLAY"
Check1 Top = 2040
Check1 Left = 120
Check1 Height = 495
Check1 Width = 2415
Check1 BackColor = &H80000005&
Check2 Caption = "&STOP MOVING LADDERS!!!"

Check2 Top = 1560

Check2 Left = 120

Check2 Height = 495

Check2 Width = 2415

Check2 BackColor = &H80000005&

Now Form1 would look like Screenshot: 30

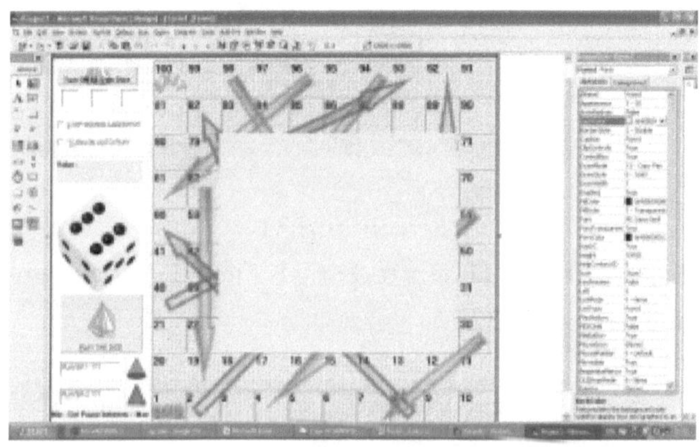

Screenshot: 30

Now we shall add another control Horizontal Scroll Bar named HScroll1 to Form1 with below properties:

HScroll1 Height = 255

HScroll1 LargeChange = 10

HScroll1 Left = 240

HScroll1 Max = 100

HScroll1 Min = 0

HScroll1 SmallChange = 1

HScroll1 Top = 9720

HScroll1 Value = 0

HScroll1 Width = 2295

Now Form1 would look like Screenshot: 31

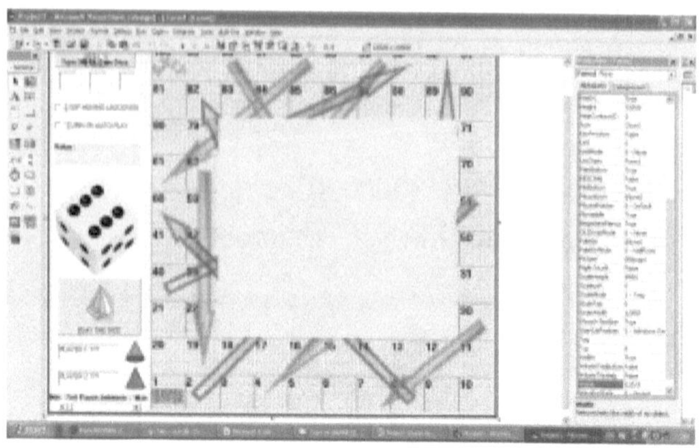

Screenshot: 31

Now we shall add three Timers to Form1 Timer1, Timer2 and Timer3 as shown in Screenshot: 32

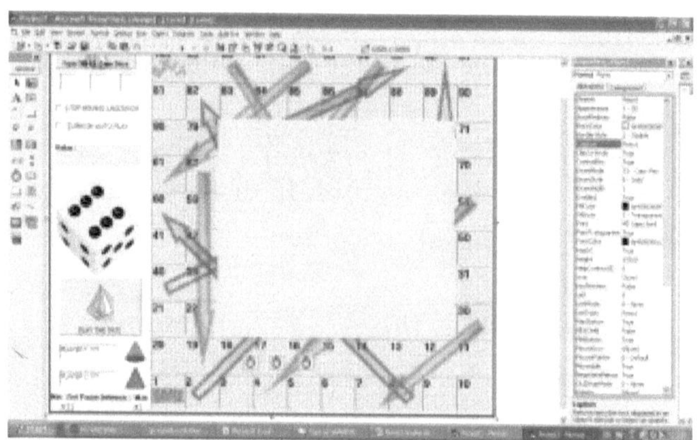

Screenshot: 32

Set below properties to Timers

    Timer1 Enabled = False

    Timer1 Interval = 50

    Timer1 Left = any value like 0 or 100 etc

    Timer1 Top = any value like 0 or 100 etc

    Timer2 Enabled = False

Timer2 Interval = 500

Timer2 Left = any value like 0 or 100 etc

Timer2 Top = any value like 0 or 100 etc

Timer3 Enabled = True

Timer3 Interval = 1000

Timer3 Left = any value like 0 or 100 etc

Timer3 Top = any value like 0 or 100 etc

Now we shall make two auto moving Ladders by adding array of 18 Shapes (Rectangle) named Shape1(0), Shape1(1)...Shape1(17) to Form1 as shown in Screenshot: 33.

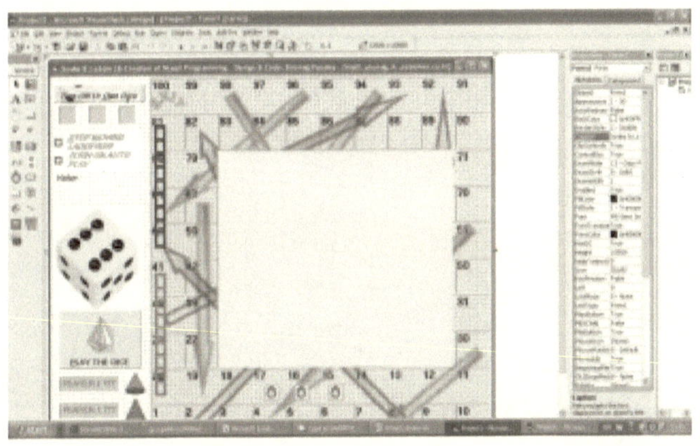

Screenshot: 33

Red Ladder is made of 9 Rectangle Shapes named Shape1(0), Shape1(1)...Shape1(8) starting lower to upper. Blue Ladder is made of 9 Rectangle Shapes named Shape1(9), Shape1(10)...Shape1(17) starting upper to lower. Set below properties to Shape1(0) to Shape1(17)

Shape1(0) Backcolor = &H80000005&

Shape1(0) BackStyle = 0 – transparent

Shape1(0) BorderStyle = 1 – Solid

Shape1(0) BorderWidth = 5

Shape1(0) Height = 375

Shape1(0) Left = 2950

Shape1(0) Shape = 0- Rectangle

Shape1(0) Width = 255

Above properties will be same for Shape1(0) to Shape1(17)

Set BorderColor property for Shape1(0) to Shape1(8) as below

Shape1(0) BorderColor = &H000000FF&

Set BorderColor property for Shape1(9) to Shape1(17) as below

Shape1(0) BorderColor = &H00FF0000&

Top property of each Shape will be different. Set this property as below:

Shape1(0) Top = 8280

Shape1(1) Top = 7920

Shape1(2) Top = 7560

Shape1(3) Top = 7200

Shape1(4) Top = 6840

Shape1(5) Top = 6480

Shape1(6) Top = 6120

Shape1(7) Top = 5760

Shape1(8) Top = 5400

Shape1(9) Top = 1400

Shape1(10) Top = 1760

Shape1(11) Top = 2120

Shape1(12) Top = 2480

Shape1(13) Top = 2840

Shape1(14) Top = 3200

Shape1(15) Top = 3560

Shape1(16) Top = 3920

Shape1(17) Top = 4280

Look at Screenshot: 34 & 35 for better understanding.

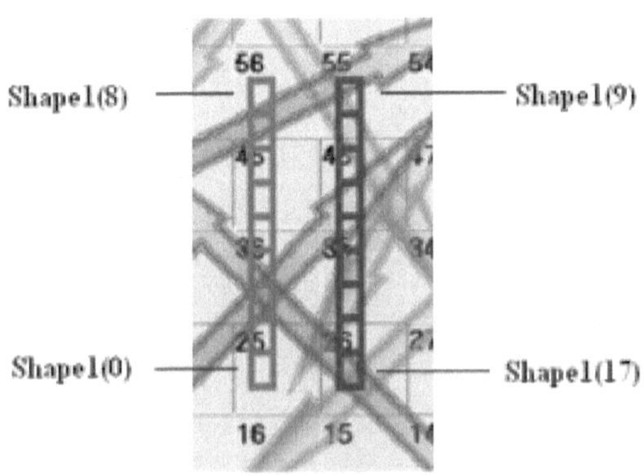

Screenshot: 34

Above two ladders are in fact shape -0 rectangle

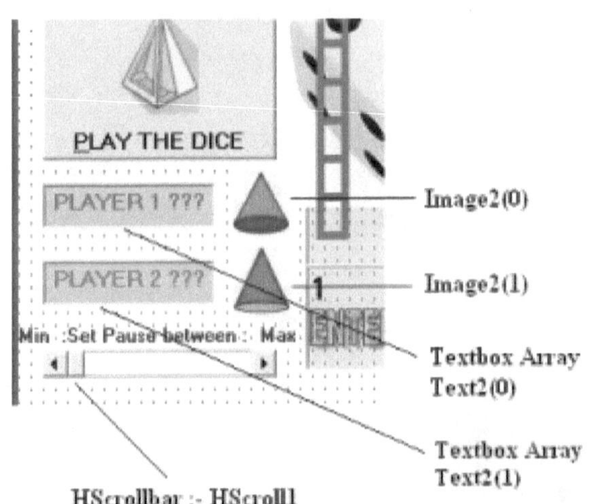

Screenshot: 35

Now we have completed the designing part. Run the Program. It will
look like as shown in Screenshot: 36:

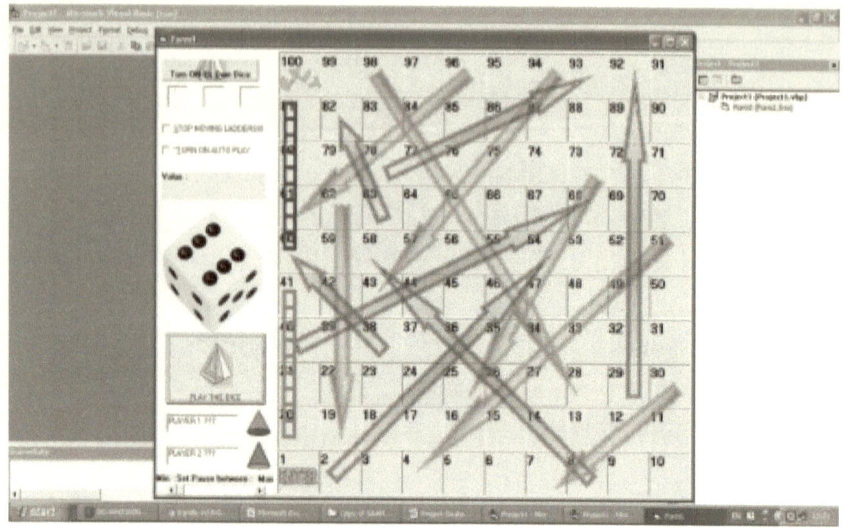

Screenshot: 36

Step 7:

Now we shall complete the coding part.

Chapter 'Code has the code.

If you have eBook then Select and Copy given Code (from **'Code** to **'End of Code**).

Go to your Visual Basic Project – Go to VIEW CODE

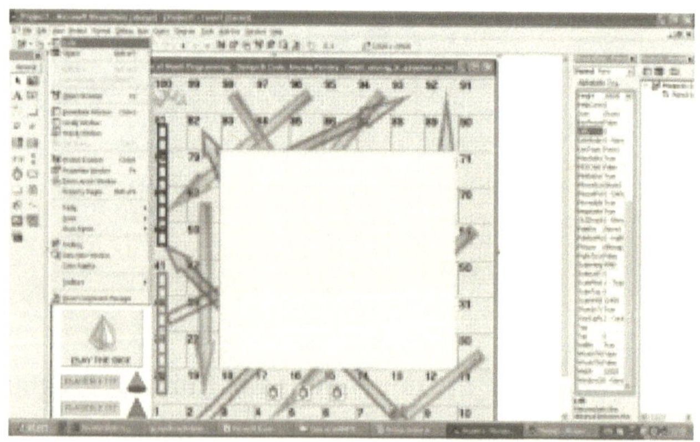

Screenshot: 37

View Code Window would be blank like Screenshot: 38

Screenshot: 38

If you have eBook then you have already selected & copied entire code. Paste the entire code in Visual Basic's Code window.

If you don't have eBook then you can type the entire code manually. Once you have done, View Code Window would look like Screenshot: 39

Screenshot: 39

Please scroll down slowly and check if there are some lines colored in red? If yes then it may be due to long code line broken into multiple lines. Please make them one line and check.

Now Save the Project. Your Visual basic Snakes & Ladders game is ready to use. Run and Check.

'Code

```
Dim CNT, P(2), G, GS1L1, GS1L2, GS2L1, GS2L2, GG, I, J, TURN, SIX, SEEDHI(13), SEEDHII(13), TURNN, NUMBERS(9, 9) As Integer
    Dim S As String
    Private Sub Check1_Click()
    If Check1.Value = 0 Then Timer2.Enabled = False
    If Check1.Value = 1 Then
    If Command1(1).Caption = "Turn OFF Ur &Own Dice" Then Command1_Click (1)
    End If
    If Check1.Value = 1 And Command1(0).Enabled = True Then Command1_Click (0)
    End Sub
    Private Sub Check2_Click()
    If Check2.Value = 1 Then
    Check2.Caption = "&MOVE THE LADDERS!!!"
    Else
    Check2.Caption = "&STOP MOVING LADDERS!!!"
    End If
    End Sub
    Private Sub Command1_Click(Index As Integer)
    If Index = 1 Then
    If Command1(1).Caption = "Turn ON Ur &Own Dice" Then
    Text1(0).Enabled = True
    Text1(0).Text = ""
    Text1(1).Text = ""
    Text1(2).Text = ""
    Text1(1).Enabled = False
    Text1(2).Enabled = False
    Check1.Value = 0
```

```
Command1(1).Caption = "Turn OFF Ur &Own Dice"
Text1(0).SetFocus
Else
Command1(1).Caption = "Turn ON Ur &Own Dice"
Text1(0).Text = ""
Text1(1).Text = ""
Text1(2).Text = ""
Text1(0).Enabled = False
Text1(1).Enabled = False
Text1(2).Enabled = False
End If
Else
If Command1(0).Caption = "PLAY AGAIN!" Then
Label1(2).Visible = False
Image2(0).Top = 8040
Image2(0).Left = 2100
Image2(1).Top = 8760
Image2(1).Left = 2100
P(0) = 0
P(1) = 0
I = 0
J = 0
G = 6
GS1L1 = 101
GS1L2 = 101
GS2L1 = 101
GS2L2 = 101
GG = 0
SIX = 0
TURNN = 0
Label1(1).Caption = ""
TURN = 0
```

```
Command1(0).Caption = Text2(TURN).Text & "! &PLAY THE DICE!"
Check1.Value = 0
Else
Timer1.Enabled = True
Command1(0).Enabled = False
End If
End If
End Sub
Private Sub Form_Load()
Label1(2).Visible = False
Image2(0).Top = 8040
Image2(0).Left = 2100
Image2(1).Top = 8760
Image2(1).Left = 2100
P(0) = 0
P(1) = 0
I = 0
J = 0
G = 6
GG = 0
GS1L1 = 101
GS1L2 = 101
GS2L1 = 101
GS2L2 = 101
SIX = 0
TURNN = 0
HScroll1.Value = 50
Label1(1).Caption = ""
TURN = 0
Command1(0).Caption = Text2(TURN).Text & "! &PLAY THE DICE!"
```

```
SEEDHI(0) = 2
SEEDHI(1) = 8
SEEDHI(2) = 29
SEEDHI(3) = 38
SEEDHI(4) = 40
SEEDHI(5) = 63
SEEDHI(6) = 78
SEEDHI(7) = 54
SEEDHI(8) = 58
SEEDHI(9) = 92
SEEDHI(10) = 60
SEEDHI(11) = 68
SEEDHI(12) = 82
SEEDHI(13) = 93
SEEDHII(0) = 98
SEEDHII(1) = 94
SEEDHII(2) = 73
SEEDHII(3) = 62
SEEDHII(4) = 51
SEEDHII(5) = 30
SEEDHII(6) = 96
SEEDHII(7) = 28
SEEDHII(8) = 43
SEEDHII(9) = 25
SEEDHII(10) = 19
SEEDHII(11) = 4
SEEDHII(12) = 7
SEEDHII(13) = 61
Jj = 0
For I = 100 To 91 Step -1
NUMBERS(0, Jj) = I
Jj = Jj + 1
```

```
Next
Jj = 0
For I = 81 To 90
NUMBERS(1, Jj) = I
Jj = Jj + 1
Next
Jj = 0
For I = 80 To 71 Step -1
NUMBERS(2, Jj) = I
Jj = Jj + 1
Next
Jj = 0
For I = 61 To 70
NUMBERS(3, Jj) = I
Jj = Jj + 1
Next
Jj = 0
For I = 60 To 51 Step -1
NUMBERS(4, Jj) = I
Jj = Jj + 1
Next
Jj = 0
For I = 41 To 50
NUMBERS(5, Jj) = I
Jj = Jj + 1
Next
Jj = 0
For I = 40 To 31 Step -1
NUMBERS(6, Jj) = I
Jj = Jj + 1
Next
Jj = 0
```

```
For I = 21 To 30
NUMBERS(7, Jj) = I
Jj = Jj + 1
Next
Jj = 0
For I = 20 To 11 Step -1
NUMBERS(8, Jj) = I
Jj = Jj + 1
Next
Jj = 0
For I = 1 To 10
NUMBERS(9, Jj) = I
Jj = Jj + 1
Next
End Sub
Private Sub Text1_Change(Index As Integer)
If Index = 0 Then
If Val(Text1(0).Text) = 6 Then
Text1(1).Enabled = True
Text1(0).Enabled = False
End If
ElseIf Index = 1 Then
If Val(Text1(1).Text) = 6 Then
Text1(2).Enabled = True
Text1(1).Enabled = False
End If
Else
If Val(Text1(2).Text) = 6 Then
Text1(2).Enabled = False
End If
End If
If Val(Text1(Index).Text) > 0 Then
```

```
CNT = 20
I = Val(Text1(Index).Text)
Command1(0).Enabled = False
Timer1.Enabled = True
End If
End Sub
Private Sub Text1_KeyPress(Index As Integer, KeyAscii As Integer)
If KeyAscii < 49 Or KeyAscii > 54 Then
KeyAscii = 8
End If
End Sub
Private Sub Text2_Change(Index As Integer)
Command1(0).Caption = Text2(TURN).Text & " &PLAY THE
DICE!"
End Sub
Private Sub Text2_Click(Index As Integer)
Text2(Index).Text = ""
End Sub
Private Sub Timer1_Timer()
GG = 10
CNT = CNT + 1
If CNT < 21 Then
Randomize
I = Int((6) * Rnd + 1)
End If
For Jj = 1 To 6
If Jj = I Then
Image1(Jj - 1).Visible = True
Else
Image1(Jj - 1).Visible = False
End If
Next
```

```
If CNT > 15 Then
Timer1.Enabled = False
If P(TURN) = 0 And SIX = 0 And I <> 6 Then I = 0
If I = 6 Then
SIX = SIX + 6
If CNT < 21 Then
CNT = 0
Timer2.Enabled = True
End If
If SIX Mod 18 = 6 Then
Label1(1).Caption = "Value of (" & Text2(TURN).Text & "): 6"
ElseIf SIX Mod 18 = 12 Then
Label1(1).Caption = "Value of (" & Text2(TURN).Text & ") : 6 +
6"
Else
Label1(1).Caption = "Value of (" & Text2(TURN).Text & ") : 0"
If Command1(1).Caption = "Turn OFF Ur &Own Dice" Then
SIX = 0
Text1(0).Text = ""
Text1(1).Text = ""
Text1(2).Text = ""
Text1(1).Enabled = False
Text1(2).Enabled = False
Text1(0).Enabled = True
Text1(0).SetFocus
End If
End If
Exit Sub
End If
SIX = SIX Mod 18
If SIX > 0 Then
If P(TURN) + I + SIX <= 100 Then
```

```
SIX = SIX + I
Label1(1).Caption = Label1(1).Caption & " + " & I
Else
SIX = 0
End If
Else
If P(TURN) + I <= 100 Then
P(TURN) = P(TURN) + I
Label1(1).Caption = "Value of (" & Text2(TURN).Text & ") : " & I
Else
I = 0
Label1(1).Caption = "Value of (" & Text2(TURN).Text & ") : 0"
End If
End If
CHAAL
GG = 0
CNT = 0
If Command1(1).Caption = "Turn OFF Ur &Own Dice" Then
Text1(0).Text = ""
Text1(1).Text = ""
Text1(2).Text = ""
Text1(1).Enabled = False
Text1(2).Enabled = False
Text1(0).Enabled = True
Text1(0).SetFocus
End If
If Check1.Value = 1 And Command1(0).Enabled = True And
Command1(0).Caption <> "PLAY AGAIN!" Then
    Timer2.Enabled = True
End If
Exit Sub
End If
```

```
End Sub
Function CHAAL()
Timer3.Enabled = False
If P(TURN) > 0 Or SIX > 0 Then
While (SIX > 5)
If Image2(TURN).Left < 2950 Then
Jj = 1
Else
Jj = 6
End If
Image2(TURN).Top = 9300 - Int((P(TURN) - 1 + Jj) / 10) * 1000
If Int((P(TURN) - 1 + Jj) / 10) Mod 2 = 0 Then
Image2(TURN).Left = 2950 + ((P(TURN) - 1 + Jj) Mod 10) * 970
ElseIf (P(TURN) - 1 + Jj) = 20 Or (P(TURN) - 1 + Jj) = 40 Or
(P(TURN) - 1 + Jj) = 60 Or (P(TURN) - 1 + Jj) = 80 Or (P(TURN) -
1 + Jj) = 100 Then
    Image2(TURN).Left = 2950
    Else
    Image2(TURN).Left = 2950 + (10 - ((P(TURN) + Jj) Mod 10)) *
970
    End If
    wait
    If  Image2(0).Left  =  Image2(1).Left  And  Image2(0).Top  =
Image2(1).Top Then
    Image2(1).Left = Image2(1).Left + 150
    Image2(1).Top = Image2(1).Top + 150
    End If
    SIX = SIX - 6
    If (P(TURN) + Jj) <= 100 Then P(TURN) = P(TURN) + Jj
    For K = 0 To 6
    If P(TURN) = SEEDHI(K) Or P(TURN) = SEEDHII(K) Then
    If P(TURN) = SEEDHI(K) Then
```

```
P(TURN) = SEEDHI(K + 7)
TURNN = 1
End If
If P(TURN) = SEEDHII(K) Then P(TURN) = SEEDHII(K + 7)
Image2(TURN).Top = 9300 - Int((P(TURN) - 1) / 10) * 1000
If Int((P(TURN) - 1) / 10) Mod 2 = 0 Then
Image2(TURN).Left = 2950 + ((P(TURN) - 1) Mod 10) * 970
ElseIf P(TURN) = 20 Or P(TURN) = 40 Or P(TURN) = 60 Or
P(TURN) = 80 Or P(TURN) = 100 Then
Image2(TURN).Left = 2950
Else
Image2(TURN).Left = 2950 + (10 - ((P(TURN)) Mod 10)) * 970
End If
wait
Exit For
End If
Next
Wend
If (P(TURN) + SIX) <= 100 Then P(TURN) = P(TURN) + SIX
SIX = 0
Image2(TURN).Top = 9300 - Int((P(TURN) - 1) / 10) * 1000
If Int((P(TURN) - 1) / 10) Mod 2 = 0 Then
Image2(TURN).Left = 2950 + ((P(TURN) - 1) Mod 10) * 970
ElseIf P(TURN) = 20 Or P(TURN) = 40 Or P(TURN) = 60 Or
P(TURN) = 80 Or P(TURN) = 100 Then
Image2(TURN).Left = 2950
Else
Image2(TURN).Left = 2950 + (10 - ((P(TURN)) Mod 10)) * 970
End If
For K = 0 To 6
If P(TURN) = SEEDHI(K) Or P(TURN) = SEEDHII(K) Then
If P(TURN) = SEEDHI(K) Then
```

```
P(TURN) = SEEDHI(K + 7)
TURNN = 1
End If
If P(TURN) = SEEDHII(K) Then P(TURN) = SEEDHII(K + 7)
wait
Image2(TURN).Top = 9300 - Int((P(TURN) - 1) / 10) * 1000
If Int((P(TURN) - 1) / 10) Mod 2 = 0 Then
Image2(TURN).Left = 2950 + ((P(TURN) - 1) Mod 10) * 970
ElseIf P(TURN) = 20 Or P(TURN) = 40 Or P(TURN) = 60 Or
P(TURN) = 80 Or P(TURN) = 100 Then
Image2(TURN).Left = 2950
Else
Image2(TURN).Left = 2950 + (10 - ((P(TURN)) Mod 10)) * 970
End If
Exit For
End If
Next
If  Image2(0).Left  =  Image2(1).Left  And  Image2(0).Top  =
Image2(1).Top Then
Image2(1).Left = Image2(1).Left + 150
Image2(1).Top = Image2(1).Top + 150
End If
End If
If P(TURN) = 100 Then
Label1(2).Caption = Text2(TURN).Text & " WON!!!"
Check1.Value = 0
Label1(2).Visible = True
Command1(0).Caption = "PLAY AGAIN!"
Command1(0).Enabled = True
Exit Function
End If
If TURNN = 0 Then
```

```
If TURN = 0 Then
GS1L1 = 101
GS1L2 = 101
TURN = 1
Else
GS2L1 = 101
GS2L2 = 101
TURN = 0
End If
Else
TURNN = 0
End If
Command1(0).Caption = Text2(TURN).Text & " &PLAY THE DICE!"
Command1(0).Enabled = True
Command1(0).SetFocus
Timer3.Enabled = True
End Function
Function wait()
For ii = 0 To HScroll1.Value * 600000
Jj = Jj + 1
Next
End Function
Private Sub Timer2_Timer()
J = J + 1
If J >= Int(HScroll1.Value / 10) + 1 Then
J = 0
Timer2.Enabled = False
Command1_Click (0)
End If
End Sub
Private Sub Timer3_Timer()
```

```
If GG = 0 Then
G = G + 1
If G > 1 And Check2.Value = 0 Then
G = 0
Randomize
ii = Int((4221) * Rnd) + 1400
ii = 1400 + Int((ii - 1400) / 1000) * 1000
For KK = 0 To 8
Shape1(KK).Top = ii + KK * 360
Next
Randomize
ii = Int((8551) * Rnd) + 2950
ii = 2950 + Int((ii - 2950) / 970) * 970
For KK = 0 To 8
Shape1(KK).Left = ii
Next
Randomize
ii = Int((4221) * Rnd) + 1400
ii = 1400 + Int((ii - 1400) / 1000) * 1000
For KK = 9 To 17
Shape1(KK).Top = ii + (KK - 9) * 360
Next
Randomize
ii = Int((8551) * Rnd) + 2950
ii = 2950 + Int((ii - 2950) / 970) * 970
If Shape1(0).Left = ii Then
If ii < (2950 + 9 * 970) Then
ii = ii + 970
Else
ii = ii - 970
End If
End If
```

```
For KK = 9 To 17
Shape1(KK).Left = ii
Next
End If
If P(0) = NUMBERS(Int((Shape1(0).Top - 1400) / 1000) + 1,
Int((Shape1(0).Left - 2950) / 970)) And GS1L1 <>
NUMBERS(Int((Shape1(0).Top - 1400) / 1000) + 4,
Int((Shape1(0).Left - 2950) / 970)) Then
    GS1L1 = NUMBERS(Int((Shape1(0).Top - 1400) / 1000) + 1,
Int((Shape1(0).Left - 2950) / 970))
    P(0) = NUMBERS(Int((Shape1(0).Top - 1400) / 1000) + 4,
Int((Shape1(0).Left - 2950) / 970))
    ElseIf P(0) = NUMBERS(Int((Shape1(0).Top - 1400) / 1000) +
4, Int((Shape1(0).Left - 2950) / 970)) And GS1L1 <>
NUMBERS(Int((Shape1(0).Top - 1400) / 1000) + 1,
Int((Shape1(0).Left - 2950) / 970)) Then
    GS1L1 = NUMBERS(Int((Shape1(0).Top - 1400) / 1000) + 4,
Int((Shape1(0).Left - 2950) / 970))
    P(0) = NUMBERS(Int((Shape1(0).Top - 1400) / 1000) + 1,
Int((Shape1(0).Left - 2950) / 970))
    End If
If P(1) = NUMBERS(Int((Shape1(0).Top - 1400) / 1000) + 1,
Int((Shape1(0).Left - 2950) / 970)) And GS2L1 <>
NUMBERS(Int((Shape1(0).Top - 1400) / 1000) + 4,
Int((Shape1(0).Left - 2950) / 970)) Then
    GS2L1 = NUMBERS(Int((Shape1(0).Top - 1400) / 1000) + 1,
Int((Shape1(0).Left - 2950) / 970))
    P(1) = NUMBERS(Int((Shape1(0).Top - 1400) / 1000) + 4,
Int((Shape1(0).Left - 2950) / 970))
    ElseIf P(1) = NUMBERS(Int((Shape1(0).Top - 1400) / 1000) +
4, Int((Shape1(0).Left - 2950) / 970)) And GS2L1 <>
```

```
NUMBERS(Int((Shape1(0).Top - 1400) / 1000) + 1,
Int((Shape1(0).Left - 2950) / 970)) Then
    GS2L1 = NUMBERS(Int((Shape1(0).Top - 1400) / 1000) + 4,
Int((Shape1(0).Left - 2950) / 970))
    P(1) = NUMBERS(Int((Shape1(0).Top - 1400) / 1000) + 1,
Int((Shape1(0).Left - 2950) / 970))
    End If
    If P(0) = NUMBERS(Int((Shape1(9).Top - 1400) / 1000) + 1,
Int((Shape1(9).Left - 2950) / 970)) And GS1L2 <>
NUMBERS(Int((Shape1(9).Top - 1400) / 1000) + 4,
Int((Shape1(9).Left - 2950) / 970)) Then
    GS1L2 = NUMBERS(Int((Shape1(9).Top - 1400) / 1000) + 1,
Int((Shape1(9).Left - 2950) / 970))
    P(0) = NUMBERS(Int((Shape1(9).Top - 1400) / 1000) + 4,
Int((Shape1(9).Left - 2950) / 970))
    ElseIf P(0) = NUMBERS(Int((Shape1(9).Top - 1400) / 1000) +
4, Int((Shape1(9).Left - 2950) / 970)) And GS1L2 <>
NUMBERS(Int((Shape1(9).Top - 1400) / 1000) + 1,
Int((Shape1(9).Left - 2950) / 970)) Then
    GS1L2 = NUMBERS(Int((Shape1(9).Top - 1400) / 1000) + 4,
Int((Shape1(9).Left - 2950) / 970))
    P(0) = NUMBERS(Int((Shape1(9).Top - 1400) / 1000) + 1,
Int((Shape1(9).Left - 2950) / 970))
    End If
    If P(1) = NUMBERS(Int((Shape1(9).Top - 1400) / 1000) + 1,
Int((Shape1(9).Left - 2950) / 970)) And GS2L2 <>
NUMBERS(Int((Shape1(9).Top - 1400) / 1000) + 4,
Int((Shape1(9).Left - 2950) / 970)) Then
    GS2L2 = NUMBERS(Int((Shape1(9).Top - 1400) / 1000) + 1,
Int((Shape1(9).Left - 2950) / 970))
    P(1) = NUMBERS(Int((Shape1(9).Top - 1400) / 1000) + 4,
Int((Shape1(9).Left - 2950) / 970))
```

```
ElseIf P(1) = NUMBERS(Int((Shape1(9).Top - 1400) / 1000) +
4, Int((Shape1(9).Left - 2950) / 970)) And GS2L2 <>
NUMBERS(Int((Shape1(9).Top - 1400) / 1000) + 1,
Int((Shape1(9).Left - 2950) / 970)) Then
    GS2L2 = NUMBERS(Int((Shape1(9).Top - 1400) / 1000) + 4,
Int((Shape1(9).Left - 2950) / 970))
    P(1) = NUMBERS(Int((Shape1(9).Top - 1400) / 1000) + 1,
Int((Shape1(9).Left - 2950) / 970))
    End If
    If Image2(0).Left >= 2950 Then
    Image2(0).Top = 9300 - Int((P(0) - 1) / 10) * 1000
    If Int((P(0) - 1) / 10) Mod 2 = 0 Then
    Image2(0).Left = 2950 + ((P(0) - 1) Mod 10) * 970
    ElseIf P(0) = 20 Or P(0) = 40 Or P(0) = 60 Or P(0) = 80 Or P(0)
= 100 Then
    Image2(0).Left = 2950
    Else
    Image2(0).Left = 2950 + (10 - ((P(0)) Mod 10)) * 970
    End If
    For K = 0 To 6
    If P(0) = SEEDHI(K) Or P(0) = SEEDHII(K) Then
    If P(0) = SEEDHI(K) Then
    P(0) = SEEDHI(K + 7)
    End If
    If P(0) = SEEDHII(K) Then P(0) = SEEDHII(K + 7)
    wait
    Image2(0).Top = 9300 - Int((P(0) - 1) / 10) * 1000
    If Int((P(0) - 1) / 10) Mod 2 = 0 Then
    Image2(0).Left = 2950 + ((P(0) - 1) Mod 10) * 970
    ElseIf P(0) = 20 Or P(0) = 40 Or P(0) = 60 Or P(0) = 80 Or P(0)
= 100 Then
    Image2(0).Left = 2950
```

```
Else
Image2(0).Left = 2950 + (10 - ((P(0)) Mod 10)) * 970
End If
Exit For
End If
Next
End If
If Image2(1).Left >= 2950 Then
Image2(1).Top = 9300 - Int((P(1) - 1) / 10) * 1000
If Int((P(1) - 1) / 10) Mod 2 = 0 Then
Image2(1).Left = 2950 + ((P(1) - 1) Mod 10) * 970
ElseIf P(1) = 20 Or P(1) = 40 Or P(1) = 60 Or P(1) = 80 Or P(1) = 100 Then
Image2(1).Left = 2950
Else
Image2(1).Left = 2950 + (10 - ((P(1)) Mod 10)) * 970
End If
For K = 0 To 6
If P(1) = SEEDHI(K) Or P(1) = SEEDHII(K) Then
If P(1) = SEEDHI(K) Then
P(1) = SEEDHI(K + 7)
End If
If P(1) = SEEDHII(K) Then P(1) = SEEDHII(K + 7)
wait
Image2(1).Top = 9300 - Int((P(1) - 1) / 10) * 1000
If Int((P(1) - 1) / 10) Mod 2 = 0 Then
Image2(1).Left = 2950 + ((P(1) - 1) Mod 10) * 970
ElseIf P(1) = 20 Or P(1) = 40 Or P(1) = 60 Or P(1) = 80 Or P(1) = 100 Then
Image2(1).Left = 2950
Else
Image2(1).Left = 2950 + (10 - ((P(1)) Mod 10)) * 970
```

```
End If
Exit For
End If
Next
End If
If Image2(0).Left = Image2(1).Left And Image2(0).Top = Image2(1).Top Then
Image2(1).Left = Image2(1).Left + 150
Image2(1).Top = Image2(1).Top + 150
End If
End If
End Sub
'End of Code
```

Make Exe File

Now Snakes & Ladders game is ready. You can also make exe file of this game.

Click on File Menu and click on Make Project1.exe Submenu as shown in Screenshot: 40

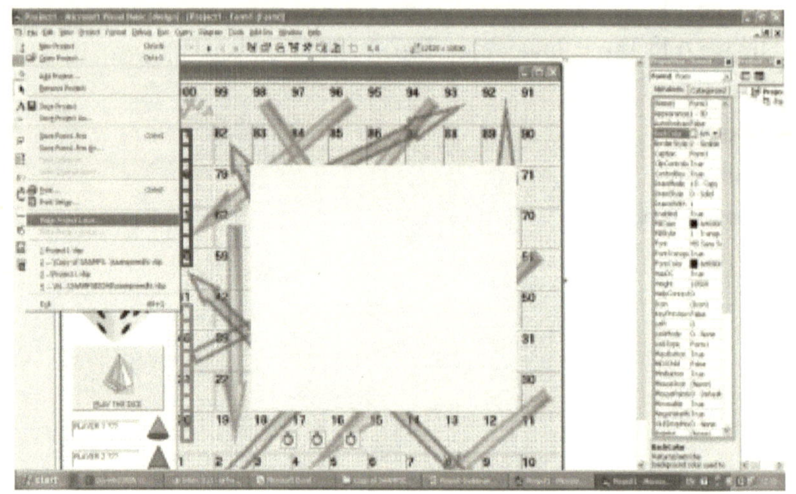

Screenshot: 40

Choose location and give a name to the exe file and then click on Ok.

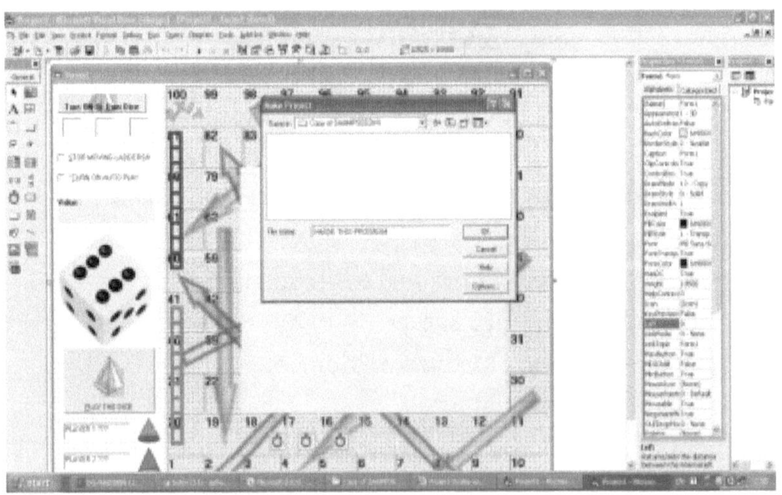

Screenshot: 41

Now exe file of Snakes & Ladders is ready and one can play this game on a Windows based computer.

Project accomplished!

Afterword

Thank you for reading "Develop Snakes & Ladders Game - Complete Guide with Code & Design". I request you to share your thoughts, experiences and your review of this book with me and readers.

Some of my books are:

Let's Play with Excel - 51 original & useful macros

Meditative Moments of a Seeker

Dhyan Bhare Lamhe - Meditative Moments

Good, Evil, Supernatural

Childhood Diamonds

Adhuri Kavitayen

Fitoor

My books are available on Amazon, Smashwords, Kobo, Apple Books, Google Play Books, Barnesandnoble, Scribd, Flipkart, Notionpress and other stores. A few links given below:

https://www.amazon.in/dp/B09VPRZHFN

https://www.amazon.in/-/hi/ANURAG-PANDEY/e/B083STJ8F8

https://play.google.com/store/books/author?id=ANURAG+S+PANDEY

https://notionpress.com/author/397403

https://www.kobo.com/us/en/ebook/meditative-moments

https://www.flipkart.com/good-evil-supernatural/p/itm49982a430f1dc

https://books.apple.com/au/author/anurag-pandey/id818684991

https://www.barnesandnoble.com/s/anurag%20pandey

https://www.smashwords.com/profile/view/ANURAGPANDEY

Or Google Anurag S Pandey. You can send me your valuable suggestions through email. You can also connect with me on Twitter and Facebook.

anuragspandey@gmail.com

https://twitter.com/ANURAGP64628371
https://www.facebook.com/anurag.pandey.98031
https://www.facebook.com/HalfCookedThoughts
Anurag S Pandey
Bhubaneswar, India

Don't miss out!

Visit the website below and you can sign up to receive emails whenever Anurag Pandey publishes a new book. There's no charge and no obligation.

https://books2read.com/r/B-A-ANUM-MMSHC

BOOKS 2 READ

Connecting independent readers to independent writers.

Did you love *Develop Snakes & Ladders Game Complete Guide with Code & Design*? Then you should read *Let's Play with Excel*[1] by Anurag Pandey!

[2]

Excel is a very powerful application. But we only use it for simple data entry purpose. We do some plus-minus and a little multiplication etc. Let's do little more with Excel. Let's play with excel. It has 51 Macros written by me. They are useful programs having original VBA coding. If you are Computer Student/ VBA Learner/ Excel Professional then you would find this book really helpful.

Dear Reader! I am Anurag Pandey. I am a writer, a poet and also a passionate programmer. I like writing codes. I used coding to automate required tasks in my office, which had reduced particular tasks completion time from hours and even days to just a few minutes. I

---

1. https://books2read.com/u/3n71Je

2. https://books2read.com/u/3n71Je

remember, once an official from Income Tax Department of India had said to me that you are an Excel expert. I had replied him that I am not an Excel expert. I only use logic in anything, if I can.

We know that Excel is a very powerful application. But we only use it for simple data entry purpose. We do some plus-minus and a little multiplication etc. and all that. Let's do a little more with Excel. Let's play with excel.

"Let's Play with Excel" has 51 Macros written by me. They are useful programs having original VBA coding. If you are Computer Student/ VBA Learner/ Excel Professional then you would find this book really helpful. I would like to tell you about a few programs of this book here.

One of its' Macro is able to give you ready to print Invoice with auto retrieving data. Another Macro is able to take details of entire class (any number of students and subjects) and to provide ready to print Mark-sheet of each student along with Result Sheet of all students at one place.

Another Macro provides you simple and easy format to enter data of one or many Invoice/s at once. Then another Macro creates JSON file from that data, which you can use for bulk upload for generating E Invoices.

Other two Macros are able to Encode/Decode data of your Excel sheet. Using this you can encode your data and can send the encoded Excel file on Mails etc. At the other hand the file can be decoded only if you have provided the Macro for decoding the sheet. You can very easily make changes in those Macros and then you would have unique Macros for encoding and decoding your Excel sheets.

Another Macro of this book has the ability to check two sheets and to list all those cells which have dissimilar data along with both the data. Using this you can check for changes in two sheets having similar data with some expected/ unexpected/ accidental/ unknown mismatches.

Some Macros from this book would help you to learn and do manipulation of data your way, some other would help you to exercise logic and programming and some other would help you to learn a little about Excel and VBA.

With great excitement and expectation, I request you to check "Let's Play with Excel" and provide your invaluable feedback.

ANURAG PANDEY

Bhubaneswar, India

Also by Anurag Pandey

Let's Play with Excel
The Mad Storyteller
◈◈◈◈ ◈◈◈◈◈◈
Meditative Moments of a Seeker
Develop Snakes & Ladders Game Complete Guide with Code &
Design